WORLD WINDOWS

Polar Bears

HEINLE
CENGAGE Learning

Y|S|G
A YBM COMPANY

Young & Son
Global, Inc.

Contents

polar bear

Arctic

ice floe

fur

paw

freeze

Polar Bears

the Arctic

Polar bears live in the Arctic.
It is cold and icy there.

How can polar bears live
in the Arctic?

Behavior

Polar bears wait near holes in the ice to catch their food.

Polar bears can swim or jump
from ice floe to ice floe.
They sometimes ride on ice floes.

Body Parts

ear

nose

Polar bears have powerful noses.
They can smell food from far away.

fur

paw

Polar bears have small, furry ears.
Their ears do not freeze in the cold.

Polar bears have thick fur.
Their fur helps them stay warm.
They sometimes roll on the ice
to clean their fur.

Polar bears have big paws.
They swim with their paws.
They are good swimmers.

How can polar bears live in the Arctic?

 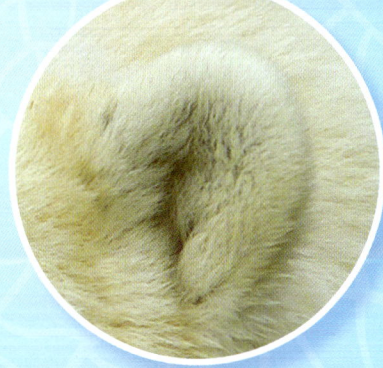

I'm a Polar Bear

I live in the Arctic. I'm a polar bear.
Here are my big paws. Here is my fur.
When I'm hungry and I look for food,
I can smell food with my nose.

I live in the Arctic. I'm a polar bear.
Here are my big paws. Here is my fur.
When I'm hungry and I look for food,
I can smell food with my nose.

Index